I0763127

A MOOD, A THOUGHT, A FEELING

A MOOD, A THOUGHT, A FEELING

INTERIORS

YOUNG HUH

FOREWORD BY ZOOEY DESCHANEL AND JONATHAN SCOTT

New York · Paris · London · Milan

For my family, for my community,
for everyone who has
dreamed of a creative life.

TABLE OF CONTENTS

FOREWORD

Home truly is where the heart feels settled. Recently, we found ourselves on a journey to create a space that felt safe and comfortable but knew that this alone would not be enough. We wanted to push our personal boundaries to realize a design that was thrilling and exciting, too, yet rooted in tradition—where every element tells a story. Creating such a narrative is where designer Young Huh shines. It takes a rare and special talent to capture and bring to life the creative whims of two exacting clients, but the collaboration was effortless. The final product is spectacular . . . and none of it would have turned out as well if we had not found Young. Her exquisite taste, ability to tell a story through design, and passion for making every moment memorable is truly magical. There is not a single detail she overlooked. She also brings a sense of calm and confidence to a generally stressful, chaotic process. Young is joyously collaborative, authentically talented, and without a doubt someone we will hold as a dear friend forever. There is much wisdom and inspiration to be gleaned from the pages of this, her first book.

—Zooey Deschanel and Jonathan Scott

INTRODUCTION

Long before interior design was my profession, it was a source of deep allure and curiosity, a beautiful, complex puzzle that I yearned to understand. To me, a gorgeous room was like a work-of-art wedding cake or a Michelin-starred meal: a sublime pleasure to experience, but a real challenge to achieve. A well-designed home looks effortless in her beauty, but what, I wondered, were her beauty secrets?

I will never forget how overwhelmed I was when I moved into my first adult home in Scarsdale, New York. I had a million ideas for what I wanted the house to look like, but no idea how to execute any of them. I was drowning in torn-out magazine pages and fabric swatches, and when my husband asked the simplest question—"Where are you going to start?"—I did not have any idea. If this feels familiar to your own early design experience, I completely understand, and we will talk about how to get started. Since that first project, I have spent twenty years in the trade of interior design and decorating, helping other families imagine and create beautiful homes. And for every project, the question that stumped me back in Scarsdale now has a clearer answer, one that can launch your process as well.

Begin by creating your own design brief. Practicalities like budget and schedule are essential to include, of course, but it is important to lead your brief with a more personal exploration. Describe yourself and what is important to you about the space(s) you are designing. What do you want your design to achieve? What impact do you want it to have? Think of all the ways you want to feel in each space, how you see yourself experiencing it. Is it a cozy, private spot, a warm, everyday gathering place, a transitional space to welcome guests with a statement of style? Do you want it to feel personal, rich with history and heirlooms? Do you want it to announce glamour, a growing art

My wildflower field that starts with mostly purple flowers and then turns yellow with goldenrod in the fall.

collection, or an evolving family? The more that these early imaginings are grounded in your own personality, your truest emotional self, the more meaningful and successful your design will be. By way of example, let me sketch out a brief of sorts for myself and this book. In all the spaces you will be seeing, I have brought to bear a lifelong and very personal love of architecture, landscape, craft, and art. My experience of design is what most informs my vision for it.

My grandparents' house in Seoul, South Korea, was surrounded by a tall imposing stone wall. Whenever I visited as a child, my heart quickened as I approached this wall, because I knew what awaited within. By the front door, there were trellised arches of currants to welcome me. In the garden itself were more arches of blossoming roses, a meticulously curated array of flowers in the ground, and a serene little fishpond. When I was six, having just read Jack and the Beanstalk, I tried planting beans of my own—here in my grandmother's magical garden, of course, where they were sure to grow. Unfortunately, I planted them in the center of a neatly raked gravel path, and as soon as my eagle-eyed grandmother spied their first shoots, she plucked them right out! At an unconscious level, this garden that I loved so much taught me my first lesson in design: a place comes to life when you feel something as you enter it, a visceral reaction that creates deep, sensory memories.

In my childhood home, I enjoyed that experience every day. When I was three, my family immigrated from Korea to Bloomfield Hills, Michigan, and our home embodied all the hope and purpose of our new American life. My mother worked hard to make every space comfortable and

ABOVE: Me age three playing in my grandparents' garden. **OPPOSITE:** My grandfather and grandmother in the garden at their house in Seoul. My grandmother is wearing a traditional Korean hanbok and my grandfather a suit, so it must have been a special occasion. I was very close to them.

lovely, and in our bright new kitchen, my father blossomed into an incredible cook.

The campus of Cranbrook Schools, where I attended middle and high school, was a design revelation. Here, I was surrounded by a glorious mix of architectural styles by Eliel Saarinen, father of Eero Saarinen, from Arts and Crafts to Finnish modernism. Every inch of the girls' school, Kingswood—from the walls to the curtains and furniture—was decorated with beautiful textiles and rugs designed by Eliel's wife, Loja. Closing my eyes, I am right back in Kingswood's beautiful green tiled lobby, the French doors to the courtyard left open in spring, the smell of flowers and mowed lawn filtering in. I remember tea being served in here, all the girls wearing Laura Ashley dresses or lacrosse uniforms. Across campus was Daffodil Hill, where tens of thousands of the namesake perennials formed rivers of yellow billowing down a sloped meadow. Whenever I take my mind back to this spot, the flowers work the same magic on me as they did on Wordsworth: my heart dances.

At Smith College, the house system suited me perfectly. I always chose to live in one of the nineteenth-century residences with dark wood floors, paneling, picture rails, and wonky staircases. Every house used Maytime china, a colorful floral pattern that no Smithie could forget. Outside, our shady lawns overlooking Paradise Pond were the perfect place to read or meet a boy from a neighboring school. In these homes and landscapes, I fell in love with the old, lived-in, and imperfect—all the things that make a space feel cozy and full of character.

I sometimes joke that maybe I did not enjoy law school because it was not very pretty. Nor was my experience working in law. Yes, the courtroom at the New York Supreme Court was gorgeous, but most of my days clerking were spent in an airless, ugly room researching legal precedence.

While practicing law, I married and had three children, which took me to Scarsdale and my

bewildering introduction to interior design. The house there became a testing ground and laboratory for my nascent interest. We have since moved to a new home (which you will see in the last section), but I still remember every room in Scarsdale and how I felt in each one. In our blue dining room with blue silk curtains, I set the table for dinner every Sunday, always with candles and flowers to give our family a feeling of celebration to start the week. Our living room, with oyster-colored walls and an overscale mirror in the center, was both a peaceful space and a lovely showcase. In the kitchen, dynamic black and white made an ideal backdrop for the room's constant buzz of activity.

Working on our home confirmed that returning to a career in law was not for me. So I landed an internship at Parsons School of Design in New York and launched my current career. My Scarsdale house ended up winning a design award, which was a clear sign I had made the right choice. The more I studied and practiced, the more I realized this trade would be a lifelong journey of learning and growing. Planning a project was rich with intellectual challenges: reviewing plans, organizing construction crews and artisans, budgeting and scheduling, keeping track of myriad details. But what mattered most, I realized, was something less tangible.

ABOVE LEFT: Kingswood, the girls' school at Cranbrook where I attended middle and high school. **ABOVE RIGHT:** My parents prior to immigrating to the United States—my father in his captain's uniform during mandatory military service, my mother in a chic two-piece outfit. **OPPOSITE:** My dining room in the Scarsdale house.

The only way I, or any of us, can achieve true beauty is through embracing and expressing the human experience. It is our capacity for feeling that imbues excitement and personality into rooms, homes, hotels, and restaurants. Our emotional selves instinctively want to connect with the built environment. In this book, I will share how moods, thoughts, and feelings have inspired my design practice, and how, by tapping into those things, you can bring beauty to your own rooms and homes as well.

As you will see, my creative process is about more than picking fabrics and finishes or an affectation. It involves connecting with something deeper and more personal in myself and in my clients. We all have access to the world of emotion within ourselves, which means this book—hopefully—can enable your own creative expression, in a way that is true to you. In Part One, we explore a variety of touchstone moods as starters for conceptualizing spaces. Part Two features three recent projects and the stories of working through the design process with my clients, all with different needs, dreams, and personalities. It is my greatest joy to help families give voice to their design imaginings. In Part Three, I share my new home in Dutchess County, New York, the result of my own unfettered creative expression. Here, I bring alive my best memories of wonderful spaces I have enjoyed in the past, and give voice to new ideas—about space and design, home, and how we live. This house is my heart, my family's favorite place to be. It is home in the fullest sense of the word, where we can be our most authentic selves. I hope this book helps you imagine and create your own truest homes, environments abundant with meaning and personality, spaces that enrich the experience of living for yourself, your loved ones, and your community—in moments and for a lifetime.

A MOOD

Why are moods so important to the design process? Recall that when I began my first project, my Scarsdale, New York, home, I did not know where to begin. I realize now that is because I was trying to reimagine an entire house, which is practically impossible all at once. Through working with my clients, I have developed a much more fruitful strategy.

Early in the process, as I get to know them, I seek an ever-deeper understanding of their most authentic stories: their personalities, history, styles—and their dreams for their home. I then tell these stories through their physical environments. Stories infuse my approach to the entire house but also its rooms and spaces. That is when moods come in. Moods can help everyone break down the design process, space by space. Some rooms will have a singular unifying mood. Other rooms will have multiple moods, with one dominant and moments of others woven in. By intently exploring an array of moods, each one layered and nuanced, you can find the inspiration to imagine a whole room, zero in on how you want rooms to be different, and more precisely articulate why you are attracted to certain colors, patterns, or design ideas.

In this section, we explore seven moods that are the root words of my design vocabulary. Not everyone's interpretation of materials and colors for moods are the same. But we can all agree on what these moods are. To lead us in, let me share three foundational questions that I ask all my clients. How do you want to feel in a space? What materials would you use to convey that feeling? What kinds of furniture, objects, or art would you want in that space to convey that feeling? These questions initiate every successful design project, and I encourage you to explore them yourselves, throughout this chapter and throughout your design journey.

CONVIVIALITY

Whenever I want to tap into the spirit of the word *convivial*, I think about its roots in Latin: *convivium*, meaning "feast." That word is derived from *convivere*, which literally translates as "to live together," but connotes far more than mundane cohabitation. "To carouse together" is its truest meaning, as in live it up! Celebrate life! In convivial spaces, we come together and relish the experience of being alive—whether it is passionate conversation and delighted laughter at a dinner party, the magical excitement of holidays, a decadent best-friends-only tasting of your vintage Sauternes in your wine room, or the spark of friendly competition in a living room backgammon tournament. Convivial spaces are not aloof; they welcome us in with a hearty hug. There is nothing ordinary about them, either. They are buzzy and electric, like an artist's salon full of the most fascinating characters and ideas.

When conceiving a convivial space, think of it as important to imagine what a gathering there might look like. How might people flow and cluster? Embracing a party's inherent sense of collectivity and improvisation, you can create a variety of seating arrangements that connect and create conversation: small spaces that gather your guests close for a game or gossip, more open areas for mingling. Convivial rooms let the party take on a life of its own. You will probably have more furniture here than in other rooms: sofas, lounge chairs, a large or multiple coffee tables, drinks tables for cocktails, varied lighting to tailor the mood. When imagining, choosing, arranging, and styling the particulars of a convivial space, I imagine myself as a discerning host and how my guests will experience the party. Cheeky artwork or a bright mix of pattern and color on the furniture can bring liveliness. Or it might be a tablescape, energized with brightly colored linens, boldly patterned dishes, and pops of lighthearted humor.

In the living room of this mountain retreat, a games table and chairs by Maxine Snider provide a festive place to play. A floor lamp by Philip Crangi and Lorin Marsh Cocoon Chairs in Rose Tarlow fabric add form and function.

ABOVE, CLOCKWISE FROM TOP: Plenty of seating surrounds a large custom coffee table by Matthew Steel, giving this mountain home living room a sense of togetherness. Artworks by Andy Warhol (left) and Billy Schenck (right). A layered table setting in cheerful colors includes dinnerware from Fete Home and Biscuit Home. Curtain fabric is by Carolina Irving and Frisée Blue Dining Chairs by Cristina Celestino. **OPPOSITE:** This party-ready living room includes a Young Huh–designed rug fabricated by Jennifer Manners, Fromental's Bamboo Lights silk wallpaper, and ample seating.

PEACEFULNESS

These are spaces that are soothing, still, and serene. They might be a refuge for you alone, to be contemplative or silent. A sunroom seat where you read with a cup of tea on a rainy day. A study with a daybed where you can lie down and brainstorm. Peaceful spaces can be shared family rooms as well—a kitchen where everyone can enjoy a quiet breakfast, say, while reading the paper. A terrace where you and your loved ones can exhale and lose yourselves in a pretty view.

When developing a color scheme, pull quiet, meditative tones. Blues and creams are many people's favorite peaceful colors, but I have clients who are soothed by deep terra-cotta red. Explore a range of colors to discover which are peaceful to you. Natural textures in fabrics and surfaces feel nurturing. Patterns with indistinct prints infuse stillness. Soft but clear lighting, clean lines, purposeful furnishings, art that is pleasing not provocative, sparing decor, and no clutter: All these things help the mind and body relax and exhale, without distraction. Bedrooms might be decorated with soft carpet, wool glacé curtains, a reading chair, and a cashmere throw. Some rooms feel peaceful if they are monochromatic, like a white kitchen, or offer a peek into nature. Think about maintaining negative space, calming openness; ask yourself: "What can I take out?" It may be removing extra objects or an unnecessary color. Certainly, there is room for standouts in the cloud: a well-placed talisman that connects you to your creativity, a portrait that delivers calming affection. Carefully crafted touches of grace, in moments, are essential to the feeling of deep peace. They remind the person enjoying the refuge—a family member, a friend, a guest, ourselves—that this space was created with loving intention, because it is essential to our well-being. They remind us that we are cared for.

A comfortable sofa by Avery Boardman is covered in a plush, pretty velvet from Clarence House—the perfect place for an afternoon nap. An artwork by Gunnar Theel is subtle and contemplative.

ABOVE, CLOCKWISE FROM TOP: A light and airy Christopher Peacock kitchen accentuates the stunning view. A custom banquette with storage by Silver Lining. A serene all-white bedroom. **OPPOSITE:** A cream leather desk and linen and sheer curtains by the Shade Store create a pacifying mood.

JOY

When I think of joy, I imagine the feeling of music, dance, creation, and expression. It is a much rarer mood than happiness, something transcendent we experience in our souls. A joyful room, then, is a very special place indeed. It could be a space for children—a bedroom or playroom—or for adult creativity: an artist's studio, a piano room, a greenhouse. It is effervescent, uplifting, a symphony of color and light, a space that makes you beam.

Designing a joyful room should feel joyful, too. Our best choices emerge not solely from our intellects, which might lead us toward contrivance or formality, but from our spirits. Give yourself freedom to improvise and honor your potential for delight and surprise. Explore paint, furniture, and details that you may have been a bit too restrained to try. Embrace exuberant, indulgent colors in unexpected combinations, irreverent juxtapositions of patterns and art. You might try a fantastic wallpaper that climbs and winds expressively, not symmetrically. Choose fabrics with bold combinations of color. Install a huge chandelier with shades painted by friends. Gather only objects that delight you. How to make the space chic and not cacophonous? Create an organized, but playful furniture plan, leaving areas for the eye to rest. If there are fabulous floors, the walls can be one color or vice versa. Whenever you use multiple patterns (particularly florals), vary their scale to create joy, rather than confusion, and mix plain, geometric, and organic. Keep your color story at the same value and follow the rule of threes: One is most dominant, the second to support, and the last are accents. In connecting your room's elements, keep your eye and heart open to the moment when they all suddenly seem to be dancing together—that is when you know you have created joy.

OPPOSITE: In a client's decoupage room, Bunny William's Azure chair and ottoman are upholstered in Josef Frank's Nippon linen fabric; the larger works of art are by Sarah Hinckley. **FOLLOWING SPREAD:** This artist's loft, in the 2019 Kips Bay Decorator Show House, is chockablock with artworks by Charles Miesmer, Bart Gulley, Judith Steinberg, Kiyoshi Otsuka, Joe Gitterman, Gunnar Theel, and Vittorio Masoni, courtesy of Cynthia Byrnes Contemporary Art.

Scalamandré

COZINESS

Why are we so drawn to cozy spaces? Why do we seem to need them? Because they hold us tight and make us feel safe. They are warm and nurturing. Chances are, when you hear the word cozy, you think of being enveloped in a blanket. Cozy spaces might be those we enjoy alone, like a hidden nook or a bedroom where we seek haven from the world. But coziness is something we can also experience together, in a library, a sunroom, or a media room.

What goes into a cozy design? Enunciate your home's transition from the public sphere to these quiet spaces that are about time alone or with family. Choose thoroughly comfortable furniture and fabrics and let your room's components come together to encourage intimacy and relaxation. You might decorate cozy spaces with colors of complex emotions that are deeper, warmer, and meditative—lush green, dark navy, neutrals. Excessive brightness can spoil the magic of a hideaway; instead, lighting should be a soft embrace. There may be details in here that can only be observed up close, like the plush texture of a fabric. You might consider furnishings made in a diminutive scale just for this place. Perhaps you can add architectural details that recall the close quarters of a ship's cabin or make a soft sofa that envelops a family on four sides. Spaces do not have to be tiny to feel cozy. In large rooms, you can create coziness by upholstering walls with your favorite fabric, choosing the most comfortable chaise longue for a corner, or creating a pillow-filled window seat with pretty curtains. To draw you in and hold you, every design choice and gesture should feel like a warm hug.

OPPOSITE: Created for the 2014 Kips Bay Decorator Show House, this built-in sitting nook in teal velvet is adorned with inset Greek key passementerie and classic Hollyhock wallpaper, all by Lee Jofa. With the lacquered wainscot and gold leaf ceiling, it is a jewel box of pattern and color. **FOLLOWING SPREAD:** This ski-home media room includes a large, custom pillow-topped sectional by Stitch NYC—enough room for the entire family to cozy up. Plush carpeting underfoot is warm and inviting.

KANDERSTEG
SCHWEIZ SWITZERLAND SUISSE
THE STYLISH LIFE

LE TELEFERIQUE ST GERVAIS-MT D'ARBOIS
TOUS LES SPORTS D'HIVER
FUNICULAIRE
TÉLÉFERIQUES
PATINOIRES, TREMPLINS
ST GERVAIS-les-Bains

VERVE

Spaces with verve are where you feel stylish and confident. It may be a buzzy restaurant where simply being in the mix is incredibly exciting. It might be a fearless entry foyer with a singleness of purpose: to dazzle. It is a room that wants to be the center of attention, the interior equivalent of taking a turn down a catwalk.

Most rooms need at least a moment of theatricality to excite us. Sometimes an entire room is created for no practical reason but rather just to be gorgeous and inspiring. Large or small, "vervacious" spaces are your opportunity to show off your most luminous, fashionable self. Entry foyers create a visitor's first impression, so instead of being a space you simply walk through, why not make it fabulous for the senses? In a dining room, you can create a striking focal point with art or glassware. A large amount of any collection always feels stylish, and placing objects against a high-contrasting color expresses a sense of daring. Powder rooms are the perfect spot to peacock with bold patterns or colors that might be too much elsewhere. Yes, rooms with verve do tend to insist that you splurge on them, but the result will be worth it. This is the place for rarified finishes, elaborate craftsmanship, and flawless artistic technique—think hand-painted silk wallpaper, eglomise to shimmer, custom wood paneling, a dramatically scaled chandelier, glossiness for the sake of glossiness. When adding art and objects to a "vervacious" space, adopt the persona of the rock star curator of a cutting-edge museum. Hang, place, and arrange boldly. Tease out fresh relationships between the pieces—sly resonances, electrifying tension. Your brief is to wow.

In this foyer, a bold and graphic mosaic tile floor—designed in-house by YHID—is paired with a textural hair-on-hide-look wallpaper by Élitis. The liveliness sets the stage for the rest of the home.

ABOVE, CLOCKWISE FROM TOP LEFT: Tonal blues create a vibrant living room; artworks by Bart Gulley and Kiyoshi Otsuka. A glimmering, glamorous powder room. A powerful pink wall color is a buzzy backdrop for artwork by Adolph Gottlieb. This orange and teal bedroom is full of drama. **OPPOSITE:** Antiques combine with modern artworks by Ellsworth Kelly and lighting by David Weeks to create a salon that is stylish and full of excitement—all courtesy of Avery & Dash Collections.

ROMANCE

For me, romantic interiors are not necessarily about love and young lovers. I use the word to describe environments that embrace fragility, unabashed prettiness, nostalgia, and the magic of the natural world. These rooms are rich with character and personality that hint of stories of lives past. Imagine a tucked away attic nook or a very traditional bedroom covered head to toe with floral wallpaper and pretty café curtains. A historic house with lots of vintage fabrics, buckets of flowers in a cherished old truck, or a cabinet full of bygone curiosities. Romantic rooms pull at your heartstrings.

When designing toward romance, a strong first step is to explore the history within a room and the home itself or the history you want to tell. Are there vestiges of the past that you can uncover and bring alive again? Perhaps there is an old nonfunctioning fireplace, whose original beauty you might excavate. You might refurbish old moldings and keep weathered beadboard as is or add uniquely vintage cabinetry details. Consider lovely patterned fabrics or wallpapers, such as a bolt of faded vintage chintz. Turning outside, to nature, a world of romance awaits: wildflowers, high grasses with paths mowed through, fruit trees with underplantings, and lush blowsy gardens. A room feels romantic with layers of detail that capture loveliness and are slightly underlit. But to avoid your room looking overwrought, create a disciplined, structured floor plan and include a few modern touches. Contrast classic fabric with a little Missoni or Gucci. Add a modern chair in a floral fabric. Accessorizing romantic rooms is such fun: flower arrangements with blossoms and tendrils that ramble wildly, old books, silver collected at tag sales, assorted teacups, imperfect fruit laying on countertops catching the light. While each of your room's elements can shine, true romance emerges when the whole space feels harmonious and graceful.

OPPOSITE, FOLLOWING SPREAD, AND PAGES 42–43: Floral patterns, moody contrast, ethereal elements, and sculptural pieces imbue romance in these spaces. Artworks by Stanley Boxer and Susan Vecsey, Courtesy Berry Campbell, New York.

MEANING

Meaning is personal. It connotes significance and close identification. It is the mood that represents all that is most specifically and uniquely you. And as such, it is perhaps a mood that should touch all rooms in some manner. Your entire home should be you. There is nothing more delightful than seeing a room or vignette and knowing that it holds a deeper story.

We all possess objects that carry very personal meaning. These might be heirlooms containing familial and ancestral stories that tell us where we came from. Or more recent treasures that we are compelled to collect that tell us and others who we are. All of these, we know, are important enough to belong in our home. But where and how to make them most meaningful? If you have a precious handful of these things, the pleasure each gives you may compound if you cluster them: lovingly curated bookcases, a wall of family artworks, objects collected on your travels, an eccentric array of your life's ephemera. If you are blessed with an abundance of meaningful things, absolutely let them enrich, deepen, and complete the mood of every space in your home. For families who want to embrace a mix of heritages, putting disparate pieces in conversation with each other can create beautifully personal frisson. If you are without heirlooms, you can bring ancestral meaning by choosing materials or architectural details that speak to your heritage. Creating meaningful spaces is also about bringing your past into your present. Put family treasures in dialogue with new artwork. Mingle a childhood fabric with a new one. A corner cabinet of my home displays ancient Korean ceramics gifted from my parents along with contemporary ceramics from young Korean artists whom I recently discovered. For me this symbolizes the ongoing conversation between generations of makers, collectors, and families who enjoy and celebrate their stories.

A library table of curiosities in an artist's loft holds of-the-moment treasures. Antique sconces and artworks by Joe Gitterman, Joy Moser, and Dana Saulnier are installed over Fromental's Braque wall covering—the perfect place for one to pause, admire, and remember.

JACQUES GARCIA
HAUTE BOHEMIANS GREECE
The Aeneid
D.H. LAWRENCE
KIPLING
NEAR & FAR
CARLOS MOTA
HOLIDAY
THE WELL-LOVED HOUSE
THE WHITE HOUSE
From CLASSIC to CONTEMPORARY
DÉCORS BARBARES
Intérieurs marocains

OPPOSITE: In a client's primary bedroom, gold leaf wallpaper from Phillip Jeffries allows the client's very personal curation of art to shine. **ABOVE, CLOCKWISE FROM TOP LEFT:** A corner of my living room showcasing Chosun-era ceramics along with pieces from contemporary Korean artists. A Louis XVI giltwood mirror and artwork by Stephanie Snider are combined with wallpaper that pays homage to the client's cultural heritage. A family heirloom etched mirror.

A THOUGHT

We began by looking at different ways to express moods, and as much as that involves the world of emotions, it is also an intensely cerebral endeavor. All design is about rigorous thinking.

In this section, we will look at three very different entire home projects, spotlighting the role of thought. For each, I describe the process of working through a client's design brief, developing the story a client wants to tell, and creating their perfect home. Every family has distinctive needs and styles, and every home comes with unique challenges. This requires designers to refine our process for each project. While my most important responsibility is to give voice to my client's desires and sensibilities, it is not my only one. My job is also to help my clients think beyond what is familiar to them, to expose them to entirely new possibilities of space, color, light, texture, and material. I help them to see a home not only for their present but for their future.

It would be impossible for me to do any of this alone. My incredible team at YHID—with Brett Williams helming business and operations; Izzy Ackerman, design director; and all our talented architects, design associates, and interns—fuel the creative and strategic thinking needed to develop concepts, plans, and specifications. Their talents inspire me every day. Together, we experiment with and refine ideas until one emerges that we are sure will take our clients's breath away. As a team, we also work hard to ensure harmony and consistency among ideas, colors, and materials, throughout the process.

Though I communicate with my clients each step of the way, ultimately, they are taking a leap of faith in me. They trust that I understand their vision of home, and they expect me to broaden it. At the end of our journey together, they will have more than their dream home. They will have an expansive new imagination for design.

TOGETHERNESS

This young family had waited many years to get exactly the right house in which to raise their children. Patience rewarded them with a grand home in the perfect location. When they called me to design their home, they emphasized that they wanted it to look like nothing else they had seen. This family had their finger on the pulse of what was cool, they knew all the latest trends in brownstone renovations, but they wanted to chart their own course. I came to appreciate this impulse the more I got to know them. They were full of confident style and glamour, unafraid to be themselves. In other words, they had verve, which became a central component of the design brief.

Just as important to my clients was their family's collection of religious and cultural art, passed down from previous generations. Rather than grouping them together, we decided they should have pride of place and special consideration in each room—in conversation with more contemporary elements. To work with clients so enthusiastic about melding their heritage with the international conversation of design was such an honor.

We created several spaces in the home for planned togetherness, but solitude was just as crucial. I was impressed by how this very close-knit family took great care to ensure that everyone had their own en suite bedrooms as well as personal places to study or work. Grandma even has her own kitchen downstairs for when she stays with them. Perhaps, I realized, the key to great togetherness is to respect alone time as well.

The original home was a confusing network of rooms with many awkward level changes. Fearlessly, my clients agreed that we should open everything up to create a boldly modern floor plan. Entering the immense parlor floor, you are greeted by a gorgeous duo: a bronze Elan

A vestibule in textural Arte wallpaper leads to the entry, featuring a framed Indian painted textile over a bronze console by Elan Atelier and a mid-century Italian pendant. A Studio Piet Boon lounge chair upholstered in a woven Dedar pattern leads to the main living space.

Atelier console below a magnificently scaled colorful Indian textile painting. They are the perfect introduction to what you will experience in this home: color, meaning, personality, and a lot of chic. Upon a dynamic wool gold and cream rug, we placed an angled deep red velvet sofa, and eccentrically shaped chairs, interesting from every angle—all under a high gloss white ceiling.

Because this level was so large, we divided the middle dining room area with floor-to-ceiling millwork to display monumental artworks and added a floating wall to create intimacy. A glossy dining table and glass chandelier echo the sheen of the living room, but usher in a new sense of conviviality that pervades the rest of the floor. At the back of the home, a fluted marble island connects a glamorous gold and stone kitchen with a comfortable seating area for four. Here, the family envisioned another area of togetherness: lounging together while a meal is cooked, Dad serving cocktails, soundtrack courtesy of his extensive collection of vinyl.

Upstairs, his and her rooms express his and her personalities. He wanted concrete and dark wood; she wanted a glamorous prettiness and a sofa for the family to cuddle together on in the mornings. Their bathrooms meet in the middle, hers with a floral mosaic stone tile, his with masculine effect, and a shower for two between them.

On the top floor is another area of shared space and privacy. His office is grounded with a monumental wood carving. Her office required a good deal of privacy and is rather off limits. In between them is an area where the children can join their parents to study or play, sunlight streaming down through a skylight. Together time and alone time, carefully conceived everywhere, brings out the best in family life.

OPPOSITE: A moment of tactile contrast in the entry. **FOLLOWING SPREAD:** The living room is anchored by an angled sectional in Dedar velvet and floor covering by the Rug Company. Walls and ceilings covered in Lacquered Walls paper by Phillip Jeffries lend formality while encouraging light to play around the space. Bronze sculpture on pedestal by Joe Gitterman and artwork by Paul Michael Graves.

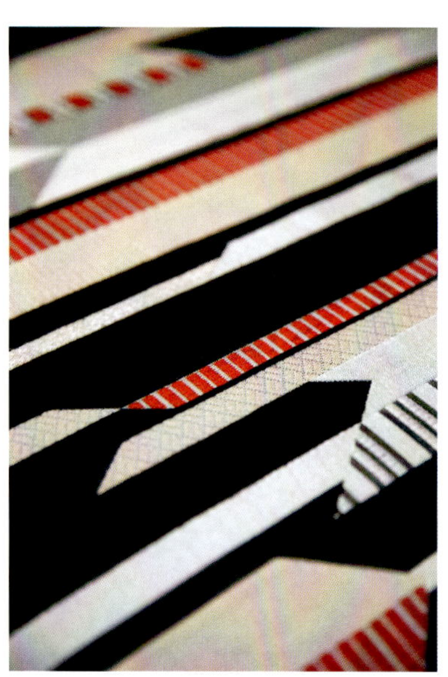

ABOVE AND OPPOSITE: Details of the living room include a Kimberly Denman chair and ottoman in Pierre Frey fabric with a lacquer table from &Tradition, a vintage François Lembo gilt and enameled ceramic mirror, Jamb mantel in Breche Serravezza marble with Marie Suri fireplace screen, and etched bronze tables by Christian Heckscher for Studio Van den Akker.

A floating wall covered in a Phillip Jeffries wallpaper provides a division between the stair and the dining space. A custom Lorin Marsh lacquer, metal, and glass dining table sits under a delicately organic John Pomp chandelier. Chairs are by Quintus with Jane Churchill fabric.

OPPOSITE: Millwork cleverly designed with closed storage and overscale openings for paintings and sculptures including a Joe Gitterman sculpture, a David Haskell vase, and a large Paul Michael Graves painting.
ABOVE: A powder room is a romantic surprise with a floating vanity with marble surround, mosaic floors, and marble wall slabs from Studium NYC offsetting a floral wallpaper.

RIGHT AND FOLLOWING SPREAD: The main kitchen is combined with a listening lounge. The bespoke sculptural island surround in fluted Paonazzo marble is a showstopper. Swiveling lounge chairs by Studio Van den Akker in a bright blue velvet lend a clubby feel. The ceiling color is Deep Caviar by Benjamin Moore.

YAYOI KUSAMA

RIGHT: The top level surprises with a daring blue-stained wood floor by Carlisle Wide Plank Floors. Clean and modern rift-sawed white oak millwork and paneling offset an antique Indian wall carving flanked by vintage lamps.
FOLLOWING SPREAD: Her primary bedroom is a jewel box of luxe and interesting finishes with paper-backed plaster panels by Holland & Sherry inset in paneling painted in Benjamin Moore's Etiquette. Here, 1950s Murano glass sconces lend additional sophistication.

ABOVE, CLOCKWISE FROM TOP LEFT: Her glamorous vanity area features a pretty skirted stool. The custom Chesney's mantel includes hand-carved art nouveau flower motifs. A cozy corner with relaxed roman shades in a soft green satin. A custom Fortuny pillow sits on the sofa. **OPPOSITE:** The bed dressed in Matouk linens under a 1960s brass and Murano glass chandelier.

ABOVE: A floral stone mosaic from Studium NYC runs from floor to ceiling on her side of the primary bathroom. **OPPOSITE:** The shared primary bath shower has slabs of Calacatta Gold marble separating "hers" and "his" areas. Her vanity is curved and glossy; shower and vanity plumbing by Lefroy Brooks.

PREVIOUS SPREAD AND ABOVE: In his primary bedroom, a wall clad in stained wood paneling hides a door to the en suite bath. The handsome bath mosaic tile is paired with THG plumbing fixtures. Hanging bedside pendants add a luminescent contrast to the concrete wall finish. **OPPOSITE:** The lounge space is a study in soothing textural differences.

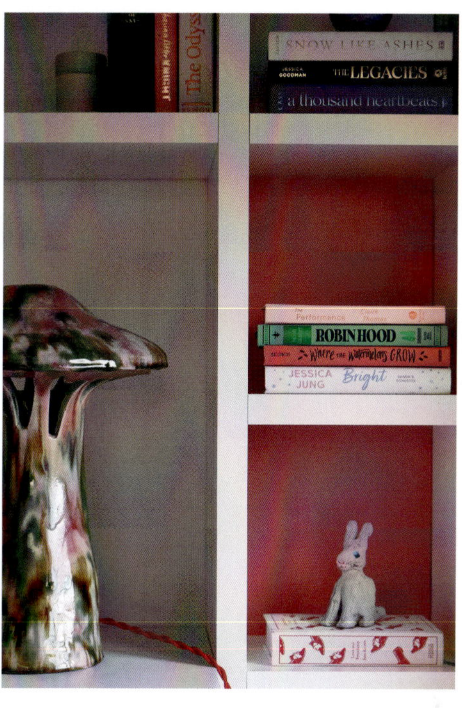

OPPOSITE AND ABOVE: The daughter's bedroom is delightfully pink with rounded furniture forms. In the girlie-glam bathroom beyond, a wall-hung vanity is topped with saturated pink onyx, and the lava stone wall tile is finished with an iridescent glaze.

Miele
Miele

PREVIOUS SPREAD, ABOVE, AND OPPOSITE: The light and bright garden-level kitchen is meant for informal gatherings. The blue and aluminum lacquer finishes and bright white Miele appliances create cheer. The built-in L-shaped banquette is perfect for breakfast or homework. The glass pendant is by Hector Finch, and the artwork is by Vinod Ray Patel.

A HOME OF ENCHANTMENTS

My clients were thrilled to move into their delightfully rambling six-level town house but were rather daunted by the fact that it required a near gut renovation. They were a young couple with small children, which was challenging enough. Their instincts to preserve as much of the original home's quirky details as possible immediately endeared them to me. When they cited Wes Anderson's *The Royal Tenenbaums* as their inspiration, it became an absolute love affair. They wanted their home to be pretty, old world, not too precious, colorful, with a modern attitude, and full of personality. The husband, a Prince fan, asked for the elevator cab to be painted bright purple. The stylish wife wanted a greenhouse feel in the kitchen with classic English cabinetry. With terraces and gardens linking the outdoors on every floor, and fascinating architectural details abounding, I was overjoyed to embark on this adventure with them.

My clients envisioned large family gatherings, parties, cozy movie nights in a screening room, playtime in the garden, cooking and eating together in the kitchen and dining room. They wanted the home to feel sociable, joyful, playful for the young children, but also have areas of calm respite. They welcomed color, pattern, and whimsy and had a taste for both antiques and modern flourishes.

Our clients wanted to enter through the classic dark wood double doors and be welcomed with cheer. Since the ground floor was not flooded with natural light, we covered the walls in a happy yellow Jean Monro wallpaper and added whimsical floral curtains. Napoleon III chairs flank the entry fireplace—I adore antique armchairs for their tiny scale and surprising comfort. She

OPPOSITE: In the entry vestibule the restored original doors are at home with a carved and limed English mirror over a Regency-style mahogany console table. The floor is the first hint of the variety of patterns to be found inside the home. **FOLLOWING SPREAD:** The large living room has multiple seating areas, framed by dramatically tall panels of Colefax and Fowler's Tree Poppy print on linen.

OPPOSITE: A Jamb mantel in Italian Breche marble sits adjacent to an antique American barley twist table and a sofa by Liberty of London. The paint color, Benjamin Moore Salisbury Green, has a glowy quality that changes throughout the day. **ABOVE:** The materials mix in the living room gives the space depth and complexity.

wanted to include family antiques in the design plan, and we also sourced more pieces from Italy to embrace her family's heritage: a vibrantly painted commode, dark wood girandoles whose finish had deepened over time, and a marble topped console for additional serving. The pieces are not only useful and pretty, but they mean something to the family.

These clients were also very modern and vivacious, eager to incorporate current fashion and style. To enliven the dining area, we hung a modern Murano glass bubble chandelier, and in other rooms, we wove in surprisingly edgy modern art. At the back of the house facing the garden is their enchanting kitchen. The children loved that the cabinet color here was named mushroom. Off the kitchen, we installed a glass and metal greenhouse-like addition, which gives the whole space a peaceful, romantic feeling.

In their sun-drenched, high-ceilinged parlor, multiple seating arrangements and a large built-in bar set the scene for big happy parties. Through that room is a moody screening room that could join the party or be closed off for cozy movie nights on a deep orange velvet sofa. The primary suite is both bright and serene, but staying true to our design's idiosyncratic spirit, we nestled in a howdah from an aunt's travels at the foot of the bed. The home had two powder rooms, which can make delightful jewel boxes full of personality. In one, we hung a classic Adelphi wallpaper and antique sconces depicting an allegory of love and friendship. In another, we installed a pink concrete sink, a meandering floral Zak+Fox wallpaper, and a gorgeous Italian mirror whose subtle green highlights contrasted nicely with our other finishes. Children's rooms can be another space for creative fun. Here, we settled on happy red stripes on the high ceilings over the tall four-poster twin beds. When I think of this family now, enjoying all these whimsical and charming spaces, I cannot help but smile. They are living their own Wes Anderson movie, full of joy.

The wet bar in the living room is perfect for parties. Custom wall shelves in Calacatta Borghini marble hold the family's assortment of Italian cocktail glasses behind an antique brass gallery rail.

MARIA
BONITA
JESÚS
REYES
LICOR DE CAFÉ
CONTRATTO
APERITIF
PATRÓN
AÑEJO TEQUILA
THE BOTANIST
22
CAMPARI

PREVIOUS SPREAD: The original oak doors and stair millwork off the garden level are made cheerful with Jean Monro striped wallpaper, trim painted in Benjamin Moore's Anjou Pear, and a Sputnik ceiling light with amethyst Murano glass globes. **ABOVE:** An antique marble-topped server is a wonderful place for display and can easily be utilized as a serving space for holiday gatherings. **OPPOSITE:** A custom built-in cabinet displays a collection of English china for easy access at the table.

The home's two powder rooms are full of pattern and special details, like the antique Queen Anne mirror with a gilded eagle detail (opposite). A peach concrete sink (above) with Vola plumbing against walls in a Zak+Fox wallpaper. The mirror above is 1920s Florentine with green painted details.

PREVIOUS SPREAD: The kitchen is all about soft light, tactile finishes, and a connection to the outside. **RIGHT:** The custom metal and glass doors and greenhouse-style atrium by All City Remodeling bring light and greenery into the romantic architecture of the space—perfect for a morning coffee. **FOLLOWING SPREAD:** The heavily figured Calacatta Viola countertops, backsplash, and upper shelf are showstoppers against the warm mushroom DeVol cabinetry and hardware.

PREVIOUS SPREAD: The garden outside the kitchen. **OPPOSITE AND ABOVE:** The primary bedroom takes advantage of the ceiling height with an eight-foot-tall headboard in a cheerful stripe. The green painted custom wood mantel and trim is Benjamin Moore Peale Green.

OPPOSITE AND ABOVE: A variety of greens and blues, warm dark woods, and a touch of orange create a palette that is both soothing and happy. Nightstand by Chaddock in Benjamin Moore Blue Dusk is placed alongside an antique English chair.

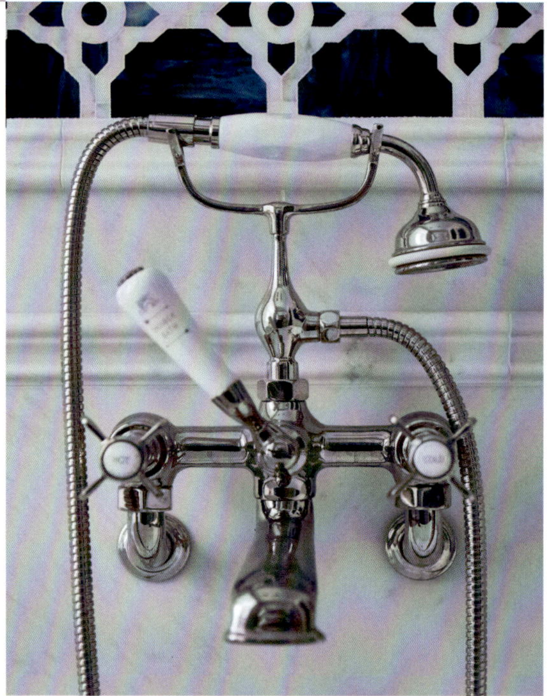

ABOVE AND OPPOSITE: Young Huh for AKDO collection tile is framed with Carrara Bella marble molding; plumbing by Lefroy Brooks. The cabinet hardware is the Serifos Snake Drop Pull by Young Huh for Modern Matter. **FOLLOWING PAGES:** Millwork walls and trim are tonal in this small guest bedroom. The guest bath was inspired by a glamorous yacht.

ABOVE AND OPPOSITE: The boys' bedroom is graphic and joyful with custom four-poster canopy beds and a striped ceiling. Classic brass hardware is a favorite detail. **FOLLOWING SPREAD:** The media room is made cozy with deep drab walls and accented with a bright orange velvet sectional. Framed photograph by Marc Cantor.

HAROLD
E MAUDE
HAROLD E MAUDE
RUTH GORDON·BUD CORT

A SHIMMERING PEACE

The prior owner of this Park Avenue residence was famous for his penchant for purchasing real estate to house his extensive collection of modern art. Though the building was beautiful, the apartment had been an uninteresting white box, more of a simple gallery space than an inviting, comfortable home. Our clients were drawn to its clean lines, and before they even closed, they were imagining their own art on its walls. When they invited me over, though I appreciated the potential for art installation, I saw a greater potential. If we could make some changes to the architecture, the space could exude élan and verve. A plain, uneven network of hallways could become a glamorous gallery. An unusually low living room ceiling was yearning to be raised, if we could open it up and see what was underneath. It is essential for designers to understand what originally draws people to a home, but our clients also rely on our vision for elevating a space—beyond what they could imagine.

Husband and wife wanted to keep mostly to creams and golds, and they were drawn to luxe materials and elegant, modern furnishings. To bring architectural interest and a unified, organized flow, we decided to add paneling detail to the gallery walls and a stepped molding in the ceiling. Installing hand-painted plum blossoms on gold leaf paper within the paneling was both quietly elegant and glamorous all at once.

An unexpected challenge arose when we broke through the living room ceiling and discovered a vast network of jogging pipes. And even though the apartment was a penthouse, we were not allowed to touch any of them. Since our clients love art, we channeled the painter Mondrian and transformed the ceiling into a pleasing field of cubes and cuboids, of varying heights and widths, which encased those wayward pipes. Underneath what we called the

The apartment's foyer and gallery glow as the light changes throughout the day, aided by gold-leafed de Gournay wallpaper. The hand-painted plum blossom pattern brings an artful sense of serenity.

Mondrian ceiling, we created a soft, welcoming contrast with curved sofas upholstered in alpaca. Curvilinear coffee tables with hand cut glass tops, some shimmering and some opaque, brought the clients' sensual bronze sculptures into rich conversation. The rug echoes the straight lines and angles of the ceiling, which completes the room's balance of organic and geometric shapes. The cream and gold color scheme may seem quite controlled, but by playing with shapes, scale, texture, and wonderful art, we have suffused the room not just with peacefulness, but with excitement and interest.

The office was an odd little room that the clients wanted to feel more intentional, architecturally integrated, and striking. We started by cladding the entire room in wood paneling, and to distract the eye from the room's lack of symmetry, we added white lacquer boxes within some of the shelves to draw the eye to a better focal point. To further imbue the room with balance, we adjusted the location of the double doors to the living room, which now gave a lovely view into the new shelves. Cladding the doors in a sunburst-shaped veneer and custom hardware created a dramatic invitation to come in and enjoy this space. In design, it is important to consider views from one room into another. When our interest is drawn from one space into another, the entire home feels connected and alive.

The primary bedroom was burdened by two low soffits, one over the only wall suitable for a king bed, and another over the dressing table area. After our trial in the living room, we knew not to try to demo these ceilings. Instead, we covered the soffits with fluted plaster, creating the effect of an extravagantly decorated tray ceiling. To echo the fluting, we upholstered the bed wall entirely in channel tufting, which lent both coziness and a deco elegance. Peaceful, poised, welcoming, and lovely—just like our clients.

OPPOSITE AND FOLLOWING PAGES: A console in goatskin and bronze serves as a sculptural counterpoint to the painted branches on the walls. The area rug is meant to suggest rippling water.
PAGES 124-125: The linear pattern of the YHID-designed Marc Phillips rug guides guests into the main entertaining space. Sculpture by Joe Gitterman and painted paper-mache artwork by Chad Schonten.

OPPOSITE, ABOVE, AND FOLLOWING: The expansive main living space juxtaposes the "Mondrian Ceiling" with a collection of curved furniture below. Custom sofas by Dune in alpaca upholstery surround nested brass coffee tables with pieced glass tops by Galerie Glustin. Mary Manning collage and Joe Gitterman bronzes via Cynthia Byrnes Contemporary Art. A view into the office from the living room. A sitting room off the gallery can convert into a guest space; artwork by Jasper Johns.

ABOVE AND OPPOSITE: The dining space features a Keith Fritz dark walnut table, a Rosie Li gingko blossom chandelier, and artwork by Laura Fayer. A DeMuro Das cabinet with cast bronze hardware details provides a visual touchpoint between the gallery, living, and dining spaces, all unified by window coverings in a Rubelli lampas.

OPPOSITE AND ABOVE: Plaster fluting and channel tufting add glamour and coziness to the primary bedroom. The sheers and curtains sparkle in the natural light. A soft rug by ALT for Living soothes at the end of the day. In a corner of the room is the perfect reading chair and artwork by Heather Sandifer.

OPPOSITE: The bed is reflected in the mirror on the lacquered vanity table. Glass objects on the table add luminosity.
ABOVE: Details of the materials used to convey a luxe, peaceful comfort.

A FEELING

Home is a sanctuary for your most authentic, idiosyncratic self. It is also an outward-facing self-expression that you share with others. In both respects, home represents your capacity to live with intentionality. Modern life is so bound by work, activity, and commitments that it is easy to lose track of what is most important to us. When you start to think about how you want your home to feel, ask yourself: How do you truly want to live? Then your ideas of home can take form, texture, and color, to create space that is singularly yours.

My husband and I had dreamed of having a home in upstate New York for years. I pictured a rambling old country house with vistas of green lawn from the kitchen window, a flower garden, lots of old trees. It would be a gathering place for our children, their friends, and ours. I imagined having parties, weekend guests, and being alone to enjoy the serenity of nature. It was a romantic fantasy.

Finally, four years ago, we started looking. One winter afternoon, we drove down a long meandering driveway lined by snow-covered old maple trees and split locust fences, across a little bridge over a stream that fed into a four-acre pond. Surrounding the pond were woodlands and open space that, in the spring, would become lush lawns. A waterfall plunged from the pond into another rushing stream. This was our country fantasy, come to life.

However, the house did not quite match that dream. I had imagined something traditional and lovingly preserved, a Hudson Valley Greek revival or gingerbread Victorian. But my husband was sure that this was the house for us, where we would live the rest of our lives and grow old. We would never find another property like this, he said. No, the house was not perfect. "But I know you can make it beautiful." His faith in me puffed me up and filled me with enthusiasm. We put in an offer that day.

MY HOME

The house was an 1820s farmhouse flanked east and west by two additions, circa the 1980s. The east was faced with brick veneer, and neither addition aligned with nor matched the original middle, where barnlike double doors had been added as an entranceway. The interior was similarly haphazard, a strange mix of folksy charm and abandoned improvements, half-painted rooms, showers I was scared to go into. The mood here was neglected.

But since we had made our decision to buy it, I immediately began to imagine how I could transform the house into our home. I spent a long time picturing how my family and I would experience and use each room, then for the next three years, poured all my creativity, love, and thought into making that vision real. The trickiest part was unifying the house's mixed architectural language. But in thinking about my own heritage—an amalgam of Korean, American, Midwest, and East Coast influences—I realized that this jumbled house could be the perfect vehicle to tell my own layered story. My father's Korean ancestry dates to the 1400s and my mother's side is so ancient it involves myths with golden eggs, whereas my family's life in America is about modernity, embracing change, and advancing into the future with hope and imagination. To capture all that, I knew I wanted modern and traditional design, Korean and American, and the global influences that are very much me as well. I also wanted to convey a vibrant narrative of place: This is a country home in beautiful, historic Dutchess County, where nature and the past surround us and where the seasons closely touch our lives.

The top priority for me and Woody Tony, my architect of fifteen years, was creating order and symmetry. The disjointed facade of brick and wood received a clapboard facelift, complete with balanced window placement, a new portico for the kitchen door, and a new door entry with

PREVIOUS SPREAD: The front of the house in fall in Benjamin Moore Simply White. **OPPOSITE:** The entry door by Dutchess Millwork is painted in Farrow & Ball Red Earth, rug by Cogolin, pendant from Charles Edwards.

sidelights. We added and moved windows and interior doors to improve the flow. Every bathroom was gutted, re-plumbed, and fitted throughout with my AKDO tile and Modern Matter hardware collection. The east and west wings were taken down to the studs to become a dream library for my husband and a modern kitchen with atrium ceiling. My intention was not to disguise these additions and make them look original to the house. All houses that have been loved for two-plus centuries have additions and changes, and I believe we should do our best to embrace the evolution.

With layout and the bones of the rooms sorted, I was excited to start decorating. This was my chance to use all the materials I had been wanting to try, to take design risks and experiment. As much as I love color, pattern, and drama, I also wanted to create a feeling of peace throughout. For beauty to be long-lasting, it needs grace and serenity. As I chose wallpapers, furniture, and lighting, I thought carefully about how colors and patterns would work and flow from one room to another. The juxtaposition of multiple layers and colors should not shock or transition abruptly. It should delight.

Eager to push the envelope as far as I could, I started with the foyer, a graciously scaled space that allowed for something dazzling. The perfect place to try something I had always dreamed of: a Korean themed wallpaper. Korean folk art is rich with colorful imagery—paintings that convey spiritual themes, allegorical renderings of animals that question the politics of class. To fill the foyer's walls with storytelling, I partnered with Fromental to create an exuberant hand-painted silk wallpaper. To complement this immersive landscape, all the period door casing and molding was repaired or re-created and painted a warm pink terra-cotta.

The oldest parts of the home were kept as is. Gaps in the two-hundred-year-old floors remained along with all the salvageable original doors and windows. I painted the living room white, as a pause between so much adjacent color. But that choice also allowed me to fill the room with lots of pattern, antiques from travels and auctions, a few modern pieces that I designed, and a mix of floral and graphic prints.

PREVIOUS PAGES AND OPPOSITE: An eighteenth-century Roman gilt console table is paired with Remains sconces and a nineteenth-century Italian mirror. Peonies in a Tiffany vase that we received as a wedding gift sit against my Soru wallpaper with Fromental.

ABOVE: A peek into the powder room with hand-painted stripes, Louis XVI mirror, custom fox faucet from PE Guerin, lava stone and Calacatta mosaic floor by YHID. **OPPOSITE:** A view into the living room from the foyer. Wool and silk rug from the Rug Company, YHID-designed pink sofa from J&P Upholstery. The tin mirror and candle sconce are from Doyle.

Throughout the design process, I was passionate about collaborating with creators. Custom work is at the center of our practice at YHID; almost anything I can imagine, our amazing team of artists, artisans, and trade partners can make. We enlisted many of these talented people to paint furniture; faux paint walls; and build, gild, and construct custom furniture, curtains, lighting, lampshades, and rugs. Their work was a beautiful expression of my profession's most steadfast truth: Designers are only as good as their artisans and trade partners.

In the upstairs bedrooms, uneven rooflines prompted me to cover walls and ceilings in wallpaper—a cozy and enveloping effect. For my own bedroom, a scheme that I had been keeping for myself for years finally came to fruition. It centered on a Madeleine Castaing fabric, Louisianne, Soane acanthus leaf print wallpaper, and a classic Cogolin rug—all coordinating with Benjamin Moore avocado green painted paneling. The mood is calm and peaceful, and I feel at one with nature.

To bring the modern architecture of the kitchen in conversation with the house's traditional parts, I paired sleek Italian Scavolini cabinetry in dark walnut and cinnamon lacquer with a moody stone backsplash and countertop, and an old-world checkered stone floor tile. Instead of one or two islands, I chose a long wood table to bathe in the sun from the new skylit atrium. The large space could have felt cold but is now inviting, warm, and convivial. For all its modernity, it feels like a country kitchen. In the second addition, we clad the library in white oak paneling with a new modern wet bar. Though the room has contemporary styling, I added small touches to make it fit within the house—a picture rail to hang art in a traditional fashion, a pair of Georgian chairs, eighteenth-century Korean tiger screens gifted from my parents. These two rooms were the most difficult to transform, but they challenged me to stretch my craft, embrace their idiosyncrasies, and make them feel like home.

PREVIOUS SPREAD: The living room has shades in embroidered Pierre Frey silk fabric, chairs in Jean Monro rose and fern, a nineteenth-century sculpture of Doryphorus, and a late eighteenth-century French School painting.
OPPOSITE: Italian neoclassical console with a European School painting, aptware lamp, and Frances Palmer vases.

ABOVE: We love views into rooms. Here the dining room looks through the living room to the entry beyond. **OPPOSITE:** In the living room a window seat with Antoinette Poisson and Chelsea Editions cushions make reading delightful. I designed the carnation rug with the Rug Company. Shown are Louis XVI fauteuils and bergères in Namay Samay and Pierre Frey fabrics. Silver altar-offering fruit from the San Francisco Fall show sit on the coffee table.

AMERICAN CIDER
A CIVIL ACTION
WOMEN FOOD

OPPOSITE: Living room looking to the dining room and the outdoors. **ABOVE, CLOCKWISE FROM TOP LEFT:** A Vittorio Masoni painting hangs above a hall table from the J. Paul Getty Museum, which serves as a bar. A lacquered box with a silver elephant from my daughter. A favorite chair upholstered in Bevilacqua velvet.

OPPOSITE: A pink Persian rug, antique wine table, and oval floral painting with carved frame ground the view into the sunroom and the outdoors beyond. **FOLLOWING SPREAD:** A corner of the sunroom with a Turkish-style banquette sofa I designed for a Kips Bay room flanked by a pair of Vaughan lamps. A circular coffee table is covered with a gorgeous suzani gifted to me by a client; the clay chicken by Julia Castillo is from the Cristina Grajales Gallery. The armchairs are covered in Cowtan & Tout Poppies, and the braided jute rug is from Stark Carpet.

RIGHT: An antique baker's table from Creel and Gow provides another surface for a collection of plants in the sunroom. Jasmine climbs over American paintings and a mirror composition. Topiaries from Orangerie mix with antique Chinese pots and delftware. **FOLLOWING SPREAD AND PAGES 166–67:** More images of the sunroom and a green potting table flanked by two George II chairs purchased at the Jasper Conran sale at Christie's. A large wash basket holds quilts for chilly nights.

DISH
COLEFAX & FOWLER

OPPOSITE: A toile cushion sits on a perfectly patinaed antique chair. **ABOVE, CLOCKWISE FROM TOP LEFT:** Ranunculus in a delft *tulipiere*; dried lavender on some of my many design books; detail of my collection of Indian wool embroidered blankets perfect for getting cozy; houseplants make a home come alive.

ABOVE: A vestibule from the dining room to the kitchen holds a happy lemon tree. On the dark navy wall are three collages from my friend, artist Stephanie Snider. A Vaughan flush-mount light adds a glimmer. **OPPOSITE:** A Louis XVI–style fauteuil upholstered in bright yellow Pavoni leather and trimmed in black-and-white Samuel & Sons Greek key tape sits against a dark green wallpaper from Élitis; the windows are dressed in Hazelton House fabric. **FOLLOWING SPREAD:** The dining room with Randolph & Hein table, Vaughan lamps, a pink Murano leaf chandelier. Élitis custom sized wallpaper panels cover a hidden door to my study.

ABOVE: I like to set my round table with multiple flower arrangements. Pink ranunculus and anemones pair well with my Wedgwood dishes. Black-and-white octagonal twist glasses from KRB combine with Baccarat wine and turquoise aperitif glasses. **OPPOSITE:** My good friends Karen and Martin at the Punctilious Mr. P's Place Cards Company created place cards for me using my dining room wallpaper. The wallpaper features a design that looks hand painted but is actually printed to scale for each wall.

ABOVE, CLOCKWISE FROM TOP LEFT: Wallpaper panel detail. Pink Murano chandelier. A view beyond the jib door to my study. Detail of the fluting and finish of a dining chair painted by Rene Escamilla. **OPPOSITE:** A view through the dining room to the living room and foyer. The dining room rug is an indigo Tabriz carpet.

PAGES 178–79, PREVIOUS PAGES, AND RIGHT: My modern country kitchen features Scavolini cabinetry, Monogram appliances including the brass hood, two sinks, and a new skylit atrium with Velux Fresh Air Skylights. The dramatic backsplash is mystic bronze marble, and the countertops are leathered dark brown granite. The refrigerator, wine fridge, and freezer are clad in a fluted lacquer. The pendants were discovered in Milan when Izzy and I happened upon the new Astier de Villatte store there.

OPPOSITE: Entering the kitchen, you see a brass rail holding vintage and antique kitchen utensils and a framed TV displaying a Thomas Cole painting. **ABOVE, CLOCKWISE FROM TOP LEFT:** The brass sink and Dornbracht durabrass faucet. The kitchen table is by Mat Steel; homey and useful accessories; close up of Astier de Villatte pendant.

ABOVE, OPPOSITE, AND FOLLOWING SPREAD: In my husband's office, the library paneling, millwork, and moldings are by Legacy Millwork and feature hardware from my Modern Matter line. A pool table separates the room's seating areas, which have a mix of mid-century and antique furnishings. A ten-foot sofa by J&P Upholstery is flanked by two framed tiger screens. An Aldo Tura coffee table with a hidden bar has a Gabriella Kiss bug sculpture that I gave my husband as an anniversary present.

ABOVE, CLOCKWISE FROM TOP LEFT: The wet bar with hidden refrigerator drawers, Lily pulls, and Victoria knobs by Modern Matter; a tiger screen with magpie; a painting by Betsy Davidson with Carl Auböck desk accessories and books below; detail of leaf bug sculpture by Gabriella Kiss.

ABOVE, CLOCKWISE FROM TOP LEFT: The wet bar is made with Fantastico Arni marble; a 200 BC Greek Aphrodite sculpture; my husband's desk is Czech deco; a tastevin from Sandra Jordan sits on a drinks table gifted to us by Steven Dailey.

PRECEDING SPREAD: The star of the show in my bedroom is the bed I designed framed in green velvet. I wanted this combination of Cogolin rug, Madeleine Castaing fabric, and Soane wallpaper for a long time. We had the tole chandelier powder coated in dark green, and the Chinese lamps provide an accent color. I do not like everything to match too perfectly. The millwork is painted in Benjamin Moore Avocado Green. **OPPOSITE:** Chairs in Décors Barbares fabric sit prettily under one of two circular windows flanking the fireplace.

OPPOSITE: The nightstands were originally brown wood. **ABOVE, CLOCKWISE FROM TOP LEFT:** Rene Escamilla painted the black-and-white designs. Detail of a gilded mirror of Orpheus with lyre and ho ho birds; corner of my bench with Clarence House fabric and Houlès trim; Cressida Bell lamps from Eerdmans.

ABOVE, OPPOSITE, AND FOLLOWING SPREAD: I wanted my primary bath to be peaceful and serene. My AKDO Stars tile in white is on the walls, and I used Waves on the floor. I fell in love with the water lily stone deck on the bathtub and knew it had to be in this bathroom. Dornbracht faucets are in durabrass gold. My Victoria and Medusa Modern Matter knobs with lapis give a glamorous detail to the vanity. A Chosun-era Korean vase, repaired in silver, holds sweet peas.

OPPOSITE AND FOLLOWING PAGES: My daughter's room was probably the primary bedroom of the original house. She insisted that I not decorate it "matchy-matchy." Walls are covered in Christopher Moore wallpaper; millwork and trims in Benjamin Moore Earthly Russet. The central feature of the room is an eighteenth-century lit à la polonaise. A pair of Louis XVI chairs are in their original fabric. A mushroom-inspired collage made for her by Stephanie Snider hangs above the mantel.

ABOVE, CLOCKWISE FROM TOP LEFT: Curtain detail fabricated by Stitch NYC with Samuel & Sons button. Andirons through Samuel Millbank; Christopher Spitzmiller lamps with Vaughan lampshades; a Hank Ehrenfried painting through Armature Projects leans on the mantel. **OPPOSITE:** An antique commode displays fanciful mushroom sculptures made by my daughter when she was little. Vintage Jansen lamp with Vaughan lampshade.

Never Let Me Go

PREVIOUS SPREAD AND OPPOSITE: Bright yellow lamps by Vaughan contrast the deep navy in my son's room. Painting by Daniel Um through Armature Projects. **ABOVE, CLOCKWISE FROM TOP LEFT:** Bathroom walls are clad in YHID lava stone and Calacatta brick. Detail of Zak+Fox's Saru paper and fabric; Waterworks fixtures have a coordinating green enamel detail; YHID lava stone and stone mosaic design.

One of my favorite views into my study features an elaborately carved antique Piedmontese mirror with urn, garlands, and cameos painted in pink and blue. Next to it is an early nineteenth-century Italian cane back painted chair in a beautiful turquoise with Manuel Canovas covered seat cushion. The wallpaper is a Mauny floral. Trims painted in Benjamin Moore Lancaster White.

ABOVE, CLOCKWISE FROM TOP LEFT: My Kaleidoscope Quilt tile pairs with Adelphi wallpaper, Fantini plumbing matches the red accents, Décors Barbares fabric with Samuel & Sons rickrack trim, detail of my AKDO tile collection. **OPPOSITE:** My study doubles as a guest room with a Resource Furniture Circe wall bed.

CROSSROADS
The Inheritance of Loss
THE NEW DAVID ESPINOZA
My Long Trip Home
BODY & SOUL
MR. MIDSHIPMAN HORNBLOWER
HER FEARFUL SYMMETRY
D.H. LAWRENCE
KIPLING
THE GREATER PERFECTION
May I Come In?

PREVIOUS SPREAD, ABOVE, AND OPPOSITE: My oldest daughter chose this Brunschwig & Fils bird and thistle pattern in aqua for her room. The room is tiny but has the benefit of an en suite bath clad in AKDO whimsy. We painted the trim to match in Benjamin Moore Blue Lake. Covering small rooms in the same pattern creates the illusion of depth. Small French chairs allow seating for my daughter and my son-in-law. The same bird and thistle fabric and bright grosgrain ribbon trim are on the Christopher Spitzmiller lamp's shade. The small side table is Regency with eglomise top purchased at the famous Mario Buatta auction. Abstract floral artwork by Bill Tansey.

IN THE GARDEN

Unlike the house, the property was love at first sight for both me and my husband. It had once been part of a six-hundred-acre dairy farm, which was sold off over the past two centuries, piece by piece. Now, we owned the original home, a large barn, a derelict caretaker's cottage, the pond, three streams, and 140 acres of land, much of which had been neglected for decades. Suddenly, we were no longer urbanites or suburbanites; we were completely in the country. As soon as our contract was signed, I bought outdoor furniture for the rear terrace. The interior would be a construction site for the foreseeable future, but I wanted my family to enjoy the outdoors right away. Umbrellas, daybeds, sofa, lounge chairs, dining table, and chairs were delivered the week we closed, while each bedroom only had mattresses on the floor.

Working on the grounds and bringing the gardens to life has been one of my greatest joys and deepest heartaches. I quickly realized that, while I could have mastery over interiors, nature has her own ideas about how things should go. Though I had long dreamed of creating an English cottage garden, I had little idea where to start. Thankfully, my friend Sam Bowman became my partner in this endeavor. On a half-acre plot of land, Sam laid out a plan against an old stone wall and potting shed. I used several pallets of leftover antique French limestone pavers to create a path between four flower beds. I found two antique decorative columns to flank the opening of the garden and four obelisks to create height and structure in each bed. Then Sam and I began choosing flowers. For spring, we planted varieties of tulips, alliums, clematis, and two miniature shaped lilac trees opposite the columns. For summer, we planted roses, foxgloves, delphiniums, and moon flowers to climb along the fence. Six raised cedar beds grow as many tomatoes, herbs, and cucumbers as we can eat. For the potting shed, I found an antique zinc table and chairs at a

OPPOSITE, FOLLOWING SPREAD, AND PAGES 224–25: French doors lead out to the rear terrace, featuring a mix of outdoor wicker furniture and tasseled umbrellas. From the terrace looking down to the pond, we watch "wildlife TV" (as we call it) every day.

PREVIOUS SPREAD: Spring brings an abundance of tulips. The old barn seems to perk up as leaves start to wake. Peonies are beginning to bud in late spring. **ABOVE AND OPPOSITE:** I wanted to tear down the potting shed, but Sam Bowman convinced me to keep it. Now it has an antique worktable and an assortment of pots that will become full of flowers and plants for the terrace and elsewhere. The old stone walls were rebuilt and repaired when we planted this garden. Metal edging, pebble gravel, and antique French limestone line the paths.

PREVIOUS SPREAD, ABOVE, AND OPPOSITE: In midsummer the wildflower fields are full, and my garden is at its peak. We load up the Kubota truck with buckets of flowers, dishes, and supplies for picnics or refreshments anywhere on the 140 acres of property. A table is set with Les Indiennes tablecloth and Adam Lippes china. Pink champagne glasses delight everyone.

As rainy days diminish, I hang curtains on the potting shed, and the wisteria grows wild. This zinc garden table, with crumbling paint and mismatched chairs, is so romantic. It is a delightful place to rest and take refreshment while gardening.

OPPOSITE: Antique watering cans not only look good but also work perfectly to water plants. Curtains add softness and color to the potting shed. **ABOVE:** An antique light and mirror add another layer of decoration. Flowers and baskets abound. Nothing brings me more joy than a bountiful crop of flowers. **FOLLOWING SPREAD:** We call this the fairy path because it is covered in ethereal blue phlox in late spring and presents the most magical walk along the stream to the stone bridge.

local dealer in Hudson, New York, and a large worktable. We added some simple curtains to the shed entrance and outfitted it with gardening tools, baskets, and an outdoor speaker—all I require to spend every possible waking moment in that garden, weeding, planting, sipping wine, and watching things grow.

Experiencing how the landscape changes over the seasons is simply magical. In the spring, baby animals appear and the first flowers bloom—snowdrops, crocuses, and daffodils. Later come tulips, lilies of the valley, and blue phlox covering paths and hills. In summer, our fields are a heaven of wildflowers—Queen Anne's Lace, buttercups, dog roses, ironweed, daisies, chicory, hyssop. Fall is the most glorious season in the Hudson Valley. My dahlias are having their moment, and the trees are ablaze with color. Fall harvests are a bounty, the farm stands exploding with apples and pumpkins. Winter is not a universally adored season in the country, but for me and my husband, it brings exhilarating life. We can boldly explore all the woods that are too brush-filled or boggy to even enter at other times of the year. We can finally follow our streams to the ends of our property. As we trek through the snow, I can easily spot abandoned nests in naked trees and shrubs, new treasures for my collection.

We love to entertain outdoors. Cocktails may be served on the terrace, tea in the wildflower meadow, or dinner by the water. I like to take our guests on a little walk around the grounds with a drink in hand. My husband offers our more adventurous visitors a ride in the Kubota. Regardless of where we are or where we set a table, I want to infuse our decor with the feeling of the season. For dishes, vases, and linens, I steer away from anything too formal or precious, instead curating an eclectic mix of things I have collected over the years. I want my guests to feel charmed and cared for but also relaxed and comfortable. In the garden, the star is nature and her beauty, and gathering friends together to enjoy the show is our greatest delight.

OPPOSITE AND FOLLOWING SPREAD: Autumn is spectacular in the Hudson Valley. Setting a table by the willow tree next to the pond with antique textiles and vintage china on a brilliantly sunny but cool fall day is perfection. Adding in pumpkins and fruit contributes to the spirit of the season.

ABOVE, CLOCKWISE FROM TOP LEFT: Dahlias are perhaps my favorite flower. Apples from the Hudson Valley are the most delicious—crisp, tart, and juicy; we find lots of feathers on the property.

ABOVE, CLOCKWISE FROM TOP LEFT: Some of my favorite things: orange dahlias; setting the table; maple leaves turning orange; floral Wedgwood china with a Laguiole olive wood knife.

With the changing of the seasons, I may swap some of the pillows to blend with the colors of the trees. An old bakery stand holds fruits of the season. The coffee table is decorated with pumpkins and my favorite dahlias that will bloom until the first frost.

ABOVE, OPPOSITE, AND FOLLOWING SPREAD: A lot of people do not like winter, but I love it. I also love snow: playing in it, walking in it. Decorating with pine garland makes me excited for Christmas. Winter means all the brush dies back and we can explore the dense woodlands. The streams look so pretty in snow. Snowy trees and a snowy house bring its own kind of magic to the garden.

RESOURCES

ANTIQUES AND ACCESSORIES
Avery & Dash Collections
averydash.com

Creel and Gow
creelandgow.com

Eerdmans New York
eerdmansnewyork.com

The Gallery at 200 Lex
nydc.com/antiques

KRB NYC
krbnyc.com

Liz O'Brien New York
lizobrien.com

Mackinnon Fine Furniture UK
mackinnonfineart.com

Matouk
matouk.com

Montage Antiques
montageantiques.com

Newel
newel.com

Red Chair on Warren
redchair-antiques.com

Samuel Milbank
samuelmilbank.com

ART
Armature Projects
armatureprojects.com

Berry Campbell Gallery
berrycampbell.com

Cristina Grajales Gallery
cristinagrajales.com

Cynthia Byrnes Contemporary Art
cynthiabyrnes.com

AUCTION HOUSES
Doyle
doyle.com

STAIR
stairgalleries.com

CARPET AND RUGS
ALT for Living
altforliving.com

Crosby Street Studios
crosbystreetstudios.com

Jennifer Manners
jennifermanners.co.uk

Marc Phillips Decorative Rugs
marcphillipsrugs.com

The Rug Company
therugcompany.com

STARK
starkcarpet.com

Studio Four NYC
studiofournyc.com

CONSTRUCTION AND BUILDING RESOURCES
All City Remodeling
allcityremodeling.com

Arthur Lange Inc.
arthurlangeinc.com

Benjamin Moore
benjaminmoore.com

California Closets
californiaclosets.com

Carlisle Wide Plank Floors
wideplankflooring.com

deVOL
devolkitchens.com

Dutchess Millwork
dutchess.com

Englebert's Moving & Delivery Service Inc.
englebertsmoving.com

Hyde Park Mouldings
hyde-park.com

Illumi-Tech
illumi-tech.com

Legacy Millworks
legacymillworksllc.com

Modern Matter
Featuring Young Huh's Jeweled Enchantress and Across the Pond collections.
modern-matter.com

Monogram
monogram.com

Resource Furniture
resourcefurniture.com

Scavolini
scavolini.com

SilverLining Inc.
silverlininginc.com

Van Go Inc.
vangoinc.net

Velux
veluxusa.com

FABRICS, WALLPAPERS, AND TRIMMINGS
Clarence House
clarencehouse.com

Cowtan & Tout
cowtan.com

de Gournay
degournay.com

Dedar
dedar.com

Élitis
elitis.fr

Fromental
Young Huh's collection includes the Soru pattern in her home's entryway.
fromental.co.uk

John Rosselli & Associates
johnrosselli.com

Kravet/Lee Jofa/Brunschwig & Fils
kravet.com

Pierre Frey
pierrefrey.com

Samuel & Sons
samuelandsons.com

Schumacher
schumacher.com

Soane Britain
soane.co.uk

ZAK+FOX
zakandfox.com

FURNITURE
Artemest
artemest.com

Built by Steel
builtbysteel.com

Dennis Miller New York
dennismiller.com

Lorin Marsh
lorinmarsh.com

Steven Dailey Studio
stevendaileystudio.com

Studio Van den Akker
studiovandenakker.com

LIGHTING
Christopher Spitzmiller Inc.
christopherspitzmiller.com

John Pomp Studios
johnpomp.com

Lutron
lutron.com

Regency Architectural Lighting
regencyny.com

Remains Lighting Co.
remains.com

The Urban Electric Company
urbanelectric.com

Vaughan Designs
vaughandesigns.com

PHILANTHROPIC ORGANIZATIONS
Asian American Pacific Islander Design Alliance
aapida.com

The Decorator's Club
thedecoratorsclub.org

Housing Works
housingworks.org

Kips Bay Decorator Show House
kipsbaydecoratorshowhouse.org

New York School of Interior Design
nysid.edu

The Olana Partnership
olana.org

PLANTS
Dutch Flower Line
nyfg.nyc

Orangerie Garden + Home
orangeriegarden.com

PLUMBING
Dornbracht
dornbracht.com

Ferguson Home
fergusonhome.com

Kohler
kohler.com

TILE AND STONE
AKDO
Featuring Young Huh's Essence and Kaleidoscope collections.
akdo.com

BAS Stone
basstonenyc.com

Studium Surface Materials
studiumnyc.com

WORKROOMS
JP Custom Upholstery
jpcustomupholstery.com

Rene Escamilla Fine Painting
@r.e.fine_painting

RoseHyll Studio
rosehyllstudio.com

Stitch NYC Inc.
stitchnycinc.com

ACKNOWLEDGMENTS

To my husband, Joon, who encouraged me to dream and to believe that anything is possible. I will love you in this life and the next and the next. To my children, Elisabeth, Oliver, Caroline, and Eliot—you are my reason for *why* every day. To my loving parents who could not have given their child more.

My YHID colleagues—I am so lucky to create beauty with you. Brett Williams, our business director, you are the heartbeat of YHID, and we would all be lost without your leadership, wisdom, and genuine kindness. Izzy Ackerman, our design director, you infuse us with the love of design every day. Thank you for all the wine and fries nights. Woody Tony—as promised, you are watching me grow old after fifteen years of working together. Thank you, Alec Strasser, Emily Rentz, Jean-Baptiste Berteloot, Angelica Malave, Ashley Sanieoff, Emeryann Hare, Tiarra Pierre-Louis, Sally Sheimo, Zac Mathias, Angel Lopez, and everyone who has come through our doors and interned, assisted, and added your passions and talents to the YHID world.

Thank you to Kathleen Jayes for making this book come alive with your gentle but thoughtful guidance. Doug Turshen and David Huang, it was an honor to witness your incredible talents in action. Tal McThenia, it has been a fun and meaningful road to write with you, my longtime friend. Thank you to Charles Miers and the entire team at Rizzoli for making my dreams come true with this book. Jill Cohen and team, thank you for getting us started.

I am so grateful to all the editors and writers who have supported us and showcased our work. Thank you to the very talented photographers and stylists who captured and made beautiful images, especially Jacob Snavely and Helen Crowther, who shot much of this book. To the best PR team ever—Elizabeth Blitzer, Nicole Nicholson, thank you for the years of support, and to Christie Tonneson and Maggie DuPré who have social media covered.

I especially want to thank all of our amazing clients who have trusted us and welcomed us into their homes and businesses. You make our daily work an honor and a joy. Thank you for letting us create beautiful environments for you. A very special thanks to those who agreed to be in this book and for allowing us to share your homes, your hopes, and your dreams. Thank you for being patient with us and for pushing us to be the best we can be.

Nick Koutoulas, Artie Lange, and Juan and Roberto Mejia, thank you for making the process of creating my home entirely creative and wonderful. It was a pleasure and a dream. To George and Alex Tsimoyianis of All City, it has been an amazing journey working on an entire chapter's worth of projects. I am grateful to my fabulous garden team led by Sam Bowman. Uriel Martinez, and Ryan Figliozzi, thank you for teaching me along the way. Margarita, we love you. Thank you to my wonderful neighbors and friends who form my community. You have filled our lives with meaning and joy, food and plants.

To all our wonderful partners and vendors, we hope to create more beauty and wonderment together! Thank you for supporting us every day in our work. Thank you for believing in us.

First published in the United States of America
in 2026 by
Rizzoli International Publications, Inc.
49 West 27th Street
New York, NY 10001
www.rizzoliusa.com

Foreword: Zooey Deschanel and Jonathan Scott
Text: Young Huh with Tal McThenia

PHOTO CREDITS
All interior images by Jacob Snavely except:
Francesco Lagnese: pages 5, 35, 36 (bottom left)
Ngoc Minh Ngo: pages 8, 24, 28-9, 30, 45
Brett Williams: pages 10, 244 (top left)
Brittany Ambridge: page 15
Lisa Flood: pages 19, 20 (top), 32-33
Nick Johnson: page 36 (top right)
Ellen McDermott, Bridget Sciales, courtesy of Avery & Dash: pages 36 (bottom right), 37
Audrey Margarite, courtesy of Lee Jofa: page 38
John Bessler: pages 40-41

Jacket:
Jacob Snavely: Front and back cover photos
Nick Carter: Author photo
Case: Design by Young Huh for Fromental
Endpapers: Design by Young Huh for Lee Jofa

ART CREDITS
Page 20 © 2025 Jasper Johns and ULAE / Licensed by VAGA at Artists Rights Society (ARS), NY, Published by Universal Limited Art Editions
Page 131 © 2025 The Andy Warhol Foundation for the Visual Arts, Inc. / Licensed by Artists Rights Society (ARS), New York

Publisher: Charles Miers
Senior Editor: Kathleen Jayes
Design: Doug Turshen with David Huang
Production Manager: Barbara Sadick
Managing Editor: Lynn Scrabis

ISBN: 978-0-8478-7632-7
Library of Congress Control Number: 2025946186

Printed in Singapore
2026 2027 2028 2029 / 10 9 8 7 6 5 4 3 2 1

The authorized representative in the EU for product safety and compliance is Mondadori Libri S.p.A., via Gian Battista Vico 42, Milan, Italy, 20123,
www.mondadori.it

Visit us online:
Instagram: @RizzoliBooks
Facebook.com/RizzoliNewYork
Youtube.com/user/RizzoliNY